# By His Wounds

# By His Wounds

**A Lenten Study Course**

Tony Castle

First published in 1998 by
KEVIN MAYHEW LTD
Buxhall
Stowmarket
Suffolk IP14 3DJ

2 3 4 5 6 7 8 9

ISBN 1 84003 267 7
Catalogue No. 1500231


Cover design by Angela Staley
Typesetting by Louise Selfe
Printed in Great Britain

# Contents

*Dedicated to*
*friends and fellow Christians*
*of Churches Together*
*in Great Wakering*
*for whom this material*
*was first written.*

# Foreword

Life is full of opportunities; some we recognise, use and benefit from, some escape us. Lent is a season of great opportunity. It is inseparable from Easter; the more we appreciate the meaning of Easter, the more we see the need to prepare well for that great celebration of the Lord's death and resurrection.

In the first three centuries of the Church's history the period of fasting and preparation lasted only three days. As Easter was the time when new converts were baptised and received into the life of the Christian community, and their period of preparation was lengthened to forty days (a period suggested by the fasts of Moses, Elijah and especially the Lord himself), so the whole Church fasted with them. The actual period was reckoned differently in different parts of the Church. For example, in the Eastern Church it was spread over seven weeks, Saturdays and Sundays being omitted. In the Western Church the strict fasting was observed for six weeks, with only Sundays being exempt. This meant, though, that Lent was only thirty-six days long. It was not until the seventh century that the days from Ash Wednesday to the First Sunday of Lent were added, to restore the season to the symbolic forty days.

We no longer fast throughout Lent. In the Catholic Church fasting has, since 1966, been restricted to Ash Wednesday and Good Friday. In the Orthodox Church, however, abstinence from meat, fish and eggs is still widely observed.

In recent times an appreciation of the value and importance of Lent as the season of opportunity for spiritual renewal and growth has developed considerably. There are innumerable places where Lenten groups meet; and many areas see this as an opportunity for ecumenical action. The material that follows originated in the large village of Great Wakering in Essex, where it was put together for use by the eight discussion groups that meet each year. In the following year it was taken up by groups in Shoeburyness and Southend. It is therefore material which has been well and truly tested and found of value.

There are five chapters, or 'weeks', because it is usual to start Lenten discussion groups in the first full week of Lent and not to meet in Holy Week. The idea is that each participant reads the full chapter *before* coming to the meeting. The group leader, after an introductory prayer, reads the summary aloud to remind the group of the content for the week. The Bible reading can be read then, or at the end of the discussion, if the group prefers, just before the closing prayer. If the Bible reading is used at the beginning (although it should be noted that the discussion pointers refer to the content of the chapter and not directly to the Bible reading) the group might like to use the alternative reading at the end.

The best closing prayer is that which springs spontaneously from the 'life' of the group, but if the leader prefers it the prayer provided might be used.

Whether this book is used by groups or individuals, by teachers for school assemblies or pastors for sermon material, I hope and pray that it will be as useful generally as it has been locally.

TONY CASTLE
GREAT WAKERING

# First week of Lent

## *Sign of love*

It was a busy Saturday afternoon in the High Street; my wife and I were in the jeweller's shop looking for a christening present for a friend's child. In front of us, waiting to be served, were a young couple looking at a display card of gold crosses. 'No', said the young woman, as a sales assistant held up for inspection a plain gold cross on a chain. 'No, I want one with a little man on it.'

My first reaction to this overheard comment was one of amusement, then, as the implications dawned, of horror and sadness. So many young people in modern Britain are growing up with no Christian knowledge and understanding. This must be the first generation since the Dark Ages not to be able even to identify the figure on the cross. That simple incident caused much pondering in me, and it reminded me of another incident that had occured a few years earlier.

My two daughters and I were travelling home together on the bus at the end of the school day. (I am a teacher at the school which, at that time, my daughters attended.) From the top of the double-decker bus we could clearly see two punk rockers (or whatever they are currently called) standing at the bus stop.

'Why is that punk rocker, with the spiky red hair, wearing a big gold cross, Dad?'

'Cor, look at what that girl with him's wearing!'

My daughters' comments revealed a little about themselves. Helena, the eldest, who was about 14 at that time, is quite interested in the relevance of religion to every day life, whereas Louise, a year younger, is much more interested in fashions and the style of clothes worn by other girls.

I had secretly hoped to get away with making no reply, but Helena repeated her question, adding, 'I bet they don't believe in anything – they shouldn't be wearing crosses.'

I tried to explain that it was not possible to judge a person's beliefs from the way she or he dressed – 'Can't judge a book by its cover,' interjected Helena. 'Nuns wear crosses,' Louise added. Helena mimicked Louise, repeating what she had said. We were about to launch into another round of adolescent bickering, so I firmly interrupted, and the bus moved on. (If only family life, particularly with teenagers, was as idyllic as some preachers and Church leaders believe it is!)

Helena had raised a valid point; the simple gold cross and the crucifix, signs of the magnificent sacrifice and immeasurable love of Jesus, have become commonplace insignia worn by many without any appreciation of their meaning. The identical cross on one person can be merely a good luck charm, while on a Religious sister or brother it is a sign of dedicated commitment.

In the late sixties, after two years in Peckham, my youth work took me to the Abbey Wood estate in South East London. My local parish church was the recently opened St David's on the estate. It still held a fresh, new atmosphere and I shall never forget my surprise when I first walked in the door. The large crucifix over the altar was not in the usual traditional style. The cross did not carry the naked figure of the crucified Christ but the fully clothed figure of a priest in red vestments, wearing a crown. At first this unsettled me and it took quite a while before I came to appreciate the message that the crucifix was conveying. In artistic fashion it was implementing one of the most powerful insights of the Second Vatican Council; namely that the Resurrection is the starting point and the very centre of our lives as Christians. Important as the historical event of the death of Christ was, it was the Resurrection which turned disaster into triumph, sorrow into joy, death into life. It was the Resurrection which made the sacrifice of Christ a living reality for today and every day.

A typical church of the Reform tradition does not display a large crucifix as a focal point, instead a simple plain cross is used. In dispensing with the sacrificial element of the Mass, the Protestant reformers placed more emphasis upon the risen Jesus. They did away with crucifixes showing the naked and tortured figure of Jesus, and in their place retained the simple unadorned cross. Such a cross can be understood as a symbol of the Resurrection; the cross is empty. Jesus is risen.

Which then is preferable? The crucifix, with its stark reminder of the torture endured by our Saviour? The empty cross, with its suggestion that the figure is not there because Christ has risen? Or a resplendent cross with Christ portrayed as priest and king? This is not a right or wrong situation, there is no need to choose, for we need them all.

For many people life is hard, very hard and no one knows when tragedy might strike. In many of life's conditions, fear, sickness, grief, coping with a physical or mental handicap and so on, the tortured figure of Christ, with its reminder of the pain he suffered, can give real comfort and reassurance and strength.

The empty cross, on the other hand, can be a positive reminder of how God raised Jesus, to be Lord and Christ, triumphant over sin and death. It is a sign of hope and that too can inspire and raise people up.

The cross which portrays Christ as priest and king has its own importance because it reminds us of the calling of Jesus of Nazareth to be not just a victim offered in sacrifice to the Father but also, as the Letter to the Hebrews makes so clear, that he was the priest too. He offered himself. By the acceptance of his gift the Father has established Jesus as Lord and King.

The naked figure on the crucifix reminds us of the human nature of Christ and the vested figure on the cross recalls his divinity. Both are equally important and necessary.

One thing is certain, the cross of Christ must not be allowed to become just another religious symbol. For example, the

11

crescent moon is recognised by all as the symbol of Islam, the shield of David (often referred to as the Star of David) is understood to represent Judaism. The cross, however, for Christians must be much more than a representation of Christianity. Unless the cross prompts at least prayer, it is in danger of becoming just another of society's empty signs; just another ornament, talisman or charm.

The bishops and church leaders who met in council at Nicea in 787 placed the crucifix, the Bible and icons on the same level of dignity, saying that each revealed something of the mystery of God and his immeasurable love for us. It is interesting to reflect that, in a general way, after that Second Council of Nicea, when gradually the church became divided into three large portions, icons became representative of the Orthodox churches; the Bible became more closely associated with the protesting reform movement and the crucifix with Catholicism. (Since 1910 and the birth of Ecumenism, Catholics have gradually rediscovered the Bible and together Protestants and Catholics have grown to understand and appreciate icons.)

One day, some time ago, in the Catholic Secondary school where I teach, I noticed that the crucifix, which had been hanging in one form room used by many different classes in the course of the week, had fallen off the wall and was jammed, waist-high, in full view, between a cupboard and the wall. The figure was partly unattached and the cross-beam of the crucifix was loose. Instinctively I went to remove it, but stopped and decided to conduct an experiment instead. I had come to some conclusions and developed a theory about the countless crucifixes and crosses around our school. This particular damaged crucifix was already dusty and I wondered how long it would be before a teacher, a pupil or cleaner noticed it. It would probably be two or three days, I thought, before it was noticed and retrieved. The room was adjacent to my own so it was no problem to keep a regular eye on it.

After eight weeks I felt I could leave it there no longer! As I entered the classroom I almost collided with our very good non-Catholic caretaker coming out. He had the crucifix in his hand. 'I noticed this the other day,' he said, 'and I've been meaning to remove it.' We chatted about it and decided it was beyond repair.

This simple incident left me wondering what has happened in modern times to respect for sacred things. The cross must not be permitted to become a shallow piece of insignia or a charm. It has been respected in the past as the icon of the revelation of the love of God. If we allow it to be, the crucifix can become the most perfect stimulus to meditation and prayer, and, as a result, a developing relationship with God.

The story is told by the co-workers of Mother Teresa of an army officer who visited a leper colony in Asia. He stopped, during the guided tour, to watch a nun dressing a leper's sores. The sight both nauseated and impressed him. Turning to the young nun, he exclaimed: 'How on earth can you do that, Sister? I wouldn't do it for a thousand pounds.'

'Well, I wouldn't do it for ten thousand pounds,' she replied calmly. Then, holding up the crucifix of her rosary, she added, 'But I would do it for him.'

The cross of Christ, with a naked tortured figure or a representation of the Resurrection, deserves, calls out for, our deepest respect. It should 'speak' to the serious Christian of the immeasurable love of the Son of God and of the only answer we have to the sufferings and injustices of this life.

# Summary

For many in our society the cross of Christ has become nothing more than just another piece of jewellery or a lucky charm. It is inadequate, for Christians, to regard the cross as merely the symbol of the Christian faith; it represents so much more for us.

The Second Council of Nicea (787) declared that the Bible, the cross and icons were to receive equal dignity, for each revealed God's immeasurable love for us.

Some ancient Christian traditions use the crucifix and some the empty cross of Christ. Each has complementary value. The crucifix calls to mind the wonderful, sacrificial love of Christ for us. The empty cross reminds us of Christ's triumph over death and of the Resurrection.

*Bible reading*

1 Corinthians 1:10-24
(Alternative Ephesians 2:14-20)

# Discussion points

1. Which tradition were you brought up with – that which used the cross or the crucifix?

2. Can you remember your thoughts about those of a different tradition?

3. Has there been any change, as time has passed, in your thinking?

4. Which should be emphasised most, the empty cross and the resurrection of Christ or the crucified figure and the sacrifice of Christ?

5. Do you have a cross or crucifix at home? How do you use it? As an ornament or a sacred sign to ward off evil or as an aid to prayer?

6. Have you any thoughts about the Council of Nicea placing the crucifix, the Bible and icons on the same level of dignity?

7. What action, if any, do you think you might take as a result of this discussion?

# Prayer

Most merciful God,
    your Son, our Lord and Saviour, Jesus Christ,
    endured for love of us the horrors of crucifixion.
He made a gift of himself to you;
    a sacrifice of obedient love.
You raised him to life,
    and the empty cross and the empty tomb
    hold for us the promise of eternal life.
May we always hold that cross in worshipful respect,
    an everlasting sign of Christ's love and obedience.
Amen.

# Second week of Lent

## _Wounds of love_

In the permissive mid-sixties I found myself responsible for a parish youth club in a tough part of Peckham, South East London. St Thomas's club met on a Friday evening and was very popular; but we were in the front line at the height of the Mod and Rocker troubles of that period and it was a difficult time. Newspaper headlines in the summer months drew attention to the continual violent clashes between Mods and Rockers at Hastings, Great Yarmouth and other seaside resorts; and the animosity simmered all year round wherever young people gathered.

We were basically a Mod club, with banks of motor scooters parked outside, but as time passed Rockers were painfully, but successfully, incorporated as members. I was fresh from college and very inexperienced in youth work. Soon after I took over the leadership of the club, in great simplicity, perhaps naïveté, I put up a large wood-carved crucifix on a side wall in a prominent position.

'That's nice,' one teenage Mod girl remarked, 'Is it yours? Shouldn't leave it there, it'll get broke or nicked.' I confirmed that it was mine and it had been an aunt's gift from her trip to Oberammergau in 1960. During the following two years, while the crucifix hung in the club, it was never touched or damaged in any way.

Mounting the crucifix upon the club wall, besides providing a focal point for a club prayer, I suppose I was also marking the territory for Christ; announcing by way of that action, 'this is a Christian club.' In doing that I was instinctively following a long tradition; but not one that reached all the way back to New Testament times, for Christian understanding and use of the sign or symbol of the cross has not always been the same. Attitudes to it have changed and developed over the centuries.

The early Christians did not reproduce the stark reality of the cross; they had no desire or need to remind themselves of the horrors of crucifixion. To execute a man in such a way was the Roman method of degrading runaway slaves and political agitators. Because the cross was such a horrific and shameful instrument of death the early followers of Christ had no wish to reproduce it artistically and would never have dreamt of wearing such a hideous symbol.

When the Emperor Constantine (c AD 310) came to the throne, because of his connection with Christianity, he stopped execution by such a brutal method. By that time Christians had started to reproduce the cross, but in a stylised form with no figure and a laurel wreath around it or above it. This was the unification of two symbols; the wreath being the familiar symbol of victory. When Roman generals returned victoriously to Rome, they entered the city in great triumph and were decorated with the victor's wreath. The Christians of Rome placed the wreath around the cross to proclaim Christ as the victor over death. Such a cross spoke of the death and resurrection of Christ.

During the Middle Ages, when the ordinary Christian's first-hand experience was not of crucifixion, but of grinding poverty and plagues that decimated whole neighbourhoods, artists began to depict Christ's agony on the cross in great detail.

In 1643 a mob of puritans tore down a cross that stood in Cheapside, London, and thus began a campaign against statues, stained glass and church wall paintings as well as crucifixes and decorated crosses. The Reformed churches, up until the twentieth century, would not use a cross liturgically in church and some still consider the crucifix as a Catholic aberration.

Tetullian, writing in AD 200, said, 'In all our actions we make on our foreheads the sign of the cross'. This ancient practice has not only been retained in the Catholic Church but also in the Orthodox Churches. This custom was surely one of the early influences upon the development, artistically, of calvaries and particularly the crucifix. Another powerful influence was the posture adopted by some Christians, especially monks, when praying with their arms outstretched in front. It was called the Orans posture and pictures of Christians praying in such a supplicant, pleading way can be seen in the wall paintings of the Roman catacombs.

The Orans posture gradually developed into the 'crossfigell' way of praying; the arms extended at the side, so that the person stood in the form of a cross. This is difficult to maintain for long so it had an ascetic side to it; it was particularly popular in monasteries founded by Irish monks. As well as in Ireland the 'crossfigell' is reported to have been used in France and Germany, at least in private prayer, right into the Middle Ages. In the minds of the Irish monks the remembrance of Moses praying on the mountain (Exodus 17:8-16), with arms outstretched, while the Israelites and the people of Amalek were fighting, linked easily and prayerfully with the posture of Christ on the cross.

The earliest recorded artistic effort to depict the scene on Calvary is on the door of St Sabina in Rome. This dates from the fifth century. The first and most skilful artist's impression on paper dates from AD 586 and is found on a page of the celebrated Syriac *Book of the Gospels* from Rubula. (This is now kept in Florence.) It appears to be from the vibrant Syriac Church that devotion to the crucified form of Jesus on the cross spread into Western Christianity.

As is so often the case in the history of the Church, it was the immense pressures experienced in European society at large that brought development and change. During the vicious wars and plagues that swept through Christendom in the fourteenth and fifteenth centuries, ordinary Christians found great comfort in their difficult lives from meditating on and praying before the figure of the crucified Christ.

21

Every club night in St Thomas's club in Peckham we would stop the record-player at 9.30 pm and interrupt table tennis and darts. Facing the crucifix I would lead a prayer which was a favourite of mine based upon the Five Wounds of Christ. After the prayer, which follows, we would have any club news and notices. At a boarding school retreat, years before, I had been given a copy of the prayer by Father Ignatius Spencer, a great-great-uncle of the late Diana, Princess of Wales.

I kiss the wounds in your sacred head,
    with sorrow deep and true.
May every thought of mine this day
    be an act of love for you.

I kiss the wounds in your sacred hands,
    with sorrow deep and true.
May every touch of my hands this day
    be an act of love for you.

I kiss the wounds on your sacred feet,
    with sorrow deep and true.
May every step I take this day
    be an act of love for you.

I kiss the wounds in your sacred side,
    with sorrow deep and true.
May every beat of my heart this day
    be an act of love for you.

Although the club was nominally Catholic, most of the young people who attended had but a tenuous connection with the Catholic Church or none at all. However, they always stood respectfully and there was only one night when there was a disturbance.

As usual I had asked the girls hanging about the record-player to halt the stream of rock music, the table tennis players to keep the plastic ball safe and a similar request was aimed at the dart players. Everyone responded fairly agreeably as usual, but a newcomer, a short lad with dark bushy hair and a black leather jacket, sitting with his back to where I was standing, in front of the crucifix, ignored my request that he stood and joined the rest of us. Instead he kicked a chair close to him. I decided that it was not prudent to make an issue of it there and then. I ignored the sullen back presented to me and said the prayer. The assistant leader then announced a few coming events. During the prayer and the notices the boy's bovver boots continued to kick adjacent chairs. When the music resumed I walked across to the lad and said something like, 'Right, if you cannot keep our club's rules you will have to go – now.' 'I want to go to the toilet,' Menyon replied. (The assistant leader had told me who he was at the end of the notices.) 'Okay,' I replied, 'then out.' I followed the lad, who must have been about five foot five tall, and around 15, to the side door that led to the gentlemen's toilets. He preceded me outside and I waited at the foot of the four steps which went up to the toilets. To my left hand (it would be Menyon's right as he came down the steps) was the four foot high wall of the coal bunker, for the heating system. After about two minutes the lad appeared. I thought nothing of it, but his right hand was tucked inside his half-open leather jacket. As he came to the bottom step he whipped out a glass bottle and swiftly smashed it on the top of the bunker wall. With no pause in his movement he drove the jagged glass edges straight at my face. It happened so suddenly and unexpectedly that I was caught completely off guard. The glass was an inch from my eyes when, like lightning, a hand and arm appeared from behind me and snatched the broken bottle away. Dave, the assistant leader, unknown to me, had just at that moment come through the door behind me and lunging forward in a split second, saved me from permanent disfigurement and perhaps the loss of my sight. The bottle smashed on the concrete path as Dave twisted the boy's arm behind his back and marched him through the club and threw him out into the street. Before Dave's departing remark, 'Don't come back', he enquired if I was going to call the police. I said 'No', but a few minutes later we did have to call them because Menyon was walking along our street systematically smashing every milk bottle on each doorstep that he could find. A tall burly policeman brought him back to the club entrance and asked, 'Do you want to charge him?' We asked that Menyon should receive a good talking to, and be sent away.

Christ's wounds were systematically and deliberately inflicted. If Menyon had succeeded with his broken bottle, my disfigurement would not have been the result of a deliberate and planned attack. He had found the bottle in the toilet and made a quick decision to use it as a weapon. When we look upon the wounds of Christ we see not just ugly disfigurement but painful wounds administered after long, deliberate and careful planning, (even as early as Mark 3:6 we read how the Pharisees and the Herodians were looking for ways to kill him) and on Christ's part consciously and freely accepted.

Menyon freely rejected the opportunity, (accepted by the other Mods and Rockers present) to stand respectfully while a prayer was said. Nothing more, in a Christian club, was expected of him. He lashed out against his exclusion because he wanted membership on his terms.

Again and again the Pharisees and teachers of the law laid traps for Jesus (Mark 3:1-6; Luke 14:1-6; Luke 20:20-26 are but a few examples). They had the opportunity of listening and responding to the Good News of Jesus, instead of which they 'lashed out' because they wanted membership of the Kingdom of God on their terms.

Devotion to the Five Wounds of Christ grew as the crucifix

came to mean more and more to Christians in the West. The first recorded meditation upon the five wounds (as distinct from all the wounds) comes from the pen of St Peter Damien (who died in 1072).

'He (Christ) is stripped of his clothing; he is beaten, bound and spat upon; his flesh is pierced by a fivefold wound; so that we may be healed from the entry of vices which reach us through the five senses.'

It was, however, the stigmata of St Francis of Assisi which really brought the devotion into great prominence. The fame of Francis and the events on Mount Alvernia in September 1224, when Francis received the mark of the nails in hands, feet and side, in a truly mysterious manner, made a great impact upon the devotional life of all European Christians. From this 'great miracle', as it was called at the time, the veneration of Christ's five wounds really dates. Mystics like St Gertrude and Blessed Henry Suso (died 1366) refer frequently in their writings to Christ's wounds as 'five signs of love'.

Before the Reformation, in England, there was a particularly deep devotion to the Wounds of Christ. It is said that the pious Henry VI of England (1422-1461) ordered his chaplain to provide him with a picture with some form of representation of the Wounds of Christ, which the King could have before him at his meals so that he could meditate in silence as he ate.

The widespread nature of the Devotion is affirmed by a popular swear word which was in common use before the Reformation. 'Zounds' was a shortened version of 'By God's wounds', just as 'Goodbye' has come to us from the words 'God be with you'.

# Summary

We all bear wounds inflicted upon us by others; Christ's severe physical wounds were deliberately and systematically inflicted. As Peter in his first letter reminds us (2:24), by those wounds we were healed. Devotion to the wounds of Christ, and all that they meant, grew in the Western Church from the eleventh century, receiving a great impetus from the renowned stigmata of St Francis of Assisi. Even up until Victorian times prayers were being written and used, linking our everyday actions with the saving wounds of Christ.

### Bible reading
John 20:24-31
(Alternative: 1 Peter 2:22-24)

# Discussion points

1. Why do Christians put a cross or crucifix up in a room, a classroom or a hall? Is there any point or is it just a superstitious gesture?

2. Some Christians prefer to use the symbol of the fish. Does that have the same or greater value?

3. Is the prayer *I kiss the wounds*, written in late Victorian times, appropriate for modern use?

4. Is the prayer ignoring the Resurrection of Christ?

5. Do you think that the whole idea of 'devotion' to the five wounds of Christ is too much like a medieval pious practice to be of value today?

6. Can you share any insight or inspiration that this week's material and discussion has led you to?

# Prayer

Use the prayer in the text above or the following.

*Prayer before a crucifix*

Good, kind and gentle Jesus,
   I kneel before you.
   I see and consider your five wounds.
   My eyes behold what David prophesied:
     'they have pierced my hands and my feet;
     they have counted all my bones.'
   Engrave upon me this image of yourself.
   Fulfil the yearnings of my heart;
     give me faith, hope and love,
     repentance for all my sins
     and a true turning to you for life.

*Traditional prayer*

# Third week of Lent _____

_____ *Love is the way*


'But it's alright if you love 'im', was the general opinion of the class of twenty-eight Year 11 girls. Only one or two sat quietly with their own thoughts. Towards the end of a presentation of traditional Christian teaching on sexual relationships, we were having a heated discussion.

At the conclusion I felt that I had only succeeded in confirming the sixteen-year-olds' suspicions that the Church was totally out of step with reality. The majority still maintained the commonly held opinions of their non-Christian peers. Traditionally educated Christian teachers and parents, like myself, feel a certain disappointment, perhaps distress, that the standards of the old days have gone. However, as Jack Dominion, the famous psychiatrist and writer, has repeatedly pointed out, among young people today there is an openness and honesty which is refreshing and encouraging. They appear to be more genuinely interested in the quality of relationships than former generations. In this, at least, there is hope.

When, with a Year 11 class of girls, I discuss, as our examination syllabus requires, the nature of love, I put on the classroom board something like this:

* I love my mum and dad
* I love strawberries
* I love my country
* I love my husband
* I love my best friend
* I love God
* I love my neighbour.

It soon becomes very evident that, when you examine the

seven statements, the word *love* means something a little different in each context. Talking it through, the class begins to appreciate how widely and sometimes inaccurately we use the word 'love'. The English language compels the one word to carry a wide range of meanings.

For example, on St Valentine's day, the daily papers are full of cryptic, romantic messages like 'Yo-Yo loves Cuddly Bear forever'. Three weeks later, in Britain, we have Mothering Sunday, or Mothers' Day, when children of all ages recall the wonderful debt of love they owe to their mothers. Cards on both occasions carry the word 'love', but obviously with a different meaning each time. Romantic love and filial love are both very important but neither is what Jesus had in mind when he said 'Love your neighbour'.

While in English we have only the one word to express all kinds of 'love', the Greek language used by the Gospel writers has no fewer than four. The noun *eros* and the verb *eran* is reserved for sexual love; this word does not appear at all in the New Testament. The noun *storge* and the verb *storgein* are used for family affection; the love between parents and children, brothers and sisters. The word most often used in Greek for love is the noun *philia* and its verb, *philein*. These words carry a feeling of warmth and mean to look on someone with affectionate regard; applied of course to the affection experienced in friendship and the 'cherishing' between husband and wife.

At first sight this could be thought to be the kind of love Jesus had in mind. The word is used several times in the Gospels when the warmth of friendship is referred to; for example it is used of the affection between Jesus and his friend Lazarus (John 11:3; 36). However, it is not used widely and the words most often used are *agape* and *agapan*. It is very interesting that *agape* is not used in classical Greek and only appears once or twice in the whole of the Old Testament, but it is used repeatedly – over 250 times – in the New Testament. The Christian writers

32

of the New Testament abandoned all the other Greek words in favour of *agape* for it was the nearest they could get to the true meaning of the message of Jesus.

Why did the New Testament writers so completely endorse one particular word to the exclusion of all others? It seems to be because the other words had acquired, with the passing of time, a certain definite connotation which made them unacceptable. For example, *eros* had become more associated with passion than love; and *storge* was limited to family affection. *Philia* was a lovely word but rather exclusive for it could only properly be used for those near and dear to us. Christianity needed an inclusive word which would embrace everyone; had not Jesus said 'Love your enemies?'

To express clearly the Good News of Jesus the New Testament writers also needed a word which demanded the involvement of the whole person, not just the emotions. The other Greek words for 'love' express an emotion or an experience that comes unsought. For example, usually we cannot help but love our parents or our children; nor can we help 'falling in love'. *Agape*, on the other hand, had to do with the will and choosing a course of action; after all people do not naturally love their enemies! Christian love, *agape*, is a deliberate principle of the mind and an achievement of the will. It is the power to love the unlovable, to care for those we do not like.

William Barclay, the Scottish Scripture scholar, explains clearly the meaning of *agape* in his *New Testament Words*. 'The supreme passage for the interpretation of the meaning of *agape* is Matthew 5:43-48. We are there bidden to love our enemies. Why? *In order that we should be like God.* And what is the typical action of God that is cited? God sends his rain on the just and the unjust and on the evil and the good. That is to say – *no matter what a man is like God seeks nothing but his highest good.'*

Of course Jesus is not asking us to have a romantic Valentine's Day love for the noisy family across the street, but if we are going to live in love (John 15:10) and be associated with him as friends, not as servants (John 15:15) we must try to respect and develop a caring concern for all around us regardless of whether we like them or not. The different kinds of love are sometimes in conflict.

Living through the ordinary everyday ups and downs of modern life, the daily stresses and joys, I believe that one of the most helpful and inspiring revelations of the New Testament is where John, the beloved disciple, tells us 'God is love'. He does not *have* love or possess *storge, philia* or even *agape*, as we do, or do not, as the case may be. It is his essential nature – that is what God is, love itself, with all its facets and human connotations. John continues, 'Anyone who lives in love lives in God and God lives in him'. What a tremendous thought! When in the course of our everyday life we encounter unselfish caring, we encounter God. John explains to his readers that 'no one has ever seen God; but as long as we love one another God will live in us'. This meeting with God, I believe, happens so frequently that our only problem is our blindness in not recognising Love (God) when we meet him.

A few years ago, at the time when I was writing the first draft of this chapter, it was a Sunday and Mother's Day. As a family we set off late in the morning, in our ageing Vauxhall, to see my wife's mother. Our journey to South London necessitated going through the Dartford Tunnel and its approach roads were jam-packed with traffic. After half-an-hour we had crept to within five hundred yards of the tunnel itself. There, in the midst of the crawling cars and trucks and impatient drivers, we broke down! With four children bouncing up and down in the back seat, delighted to have an exciting adventure, I tried desperately to get the car moving again. 'What, Lord', I prayed, 'do I do now?' With hazard lights flashing and my wife steering I began self-consciously to push the car through the held-up traffic to the hard shoulder. We had just arrived at the roadside when a large Volvo drew alongside and the bearded driver called out, 'Do you want a tow?' I was taken by surprise but quickly thanked him for his kind offer. He pulled in front and soon had a tow-rope attached. If, dear reader, you have never been towed you will not realise how helpless you feel as your powerless car rides very close behind a speeding vehicle. All you can do is steer, keep your foot poised ready to brake and pray anxiously that the car in front will not stop suddenly!

The gentleman and his family were also en route to celebrate Mother's Day but they towed us as far as they could and left us at a telephone. They had delayed their own journey, gone out of their way, endangered their car and for no other reason than that they cared. In the kindness of this Good Samaritan Volvo driver I believe we encountered God.

In what we call the Synoptic Gospels (Matthew, Mark and Luke) we read that the Good News of Jesus is concerned with the coming and establishment of the Kingdom of God. This term is often misunderstood. Despite appearances it does not refer to a place or an institution, but a condition or way of life in which God is acknowledged as being in control; God ruling, as in the popular hymn *Our God reigns*. We probably get our best understanding of 'God ruling' from the Lord's prayer when we pray 'Your Kingdom come, Your will be done'. That is, God rules in my life, reigns in my heart, when I in faith obey him.

The Synoptic Gospel writers share a common tradition; that is, the material for their Gospel accounts comes from the same background and similar sources. For example, Matthew and Luke seem to have had a copy of Mark's Gospel in front of them when they wrote and compiled their Gospels. In these three the 'Kingdom of God' is spoken of some 128 times, whereas in John's Gospel and letters the term only appears four times. In contrast, the Synoptic writers refer only a few times to the importance of love while John speaks of it sixty-nine times.

Matthew, Mark and Luke are saying that union with God

comes from accepting Christ as our King and allowing God to rule in our lives through him. John, however, does not pursue the metaphor of king and kingdom but uses instead everyone's experience of human relationships. His emphasis is upon the quality of our loving relationship with God and one another. 'God', says John, 'is *agape* 'and the meaning and purpose of life is to live in love, 'for anyone who lives in love lives in God, and God lives in him' (1 John 4:16). The target, says John, is that we should 'become as he is' (verse 17) and that will be when love has reached perfection in us.

There is no conflict between the Synoptic Gospels and John, because agape is to be found at the key places in the other accounts of the Good News. For example, the famous parable about the Last Judgement in Matthew 25:31-46 makes that quite clear. The virtuous ask the King, 'When did we see you hungry and feed you; or thirsty and give you a drink? When did we see you a stranger and make you welcome; naked and clothe you; sick or in prison and go to see you?' The King replies, 'When you did it to the least one of these brothers of mine, you did it to me'. Surely this is *agape* in action.

The love of Jesus led him to crucifixion. The gift of himself in love set the seal upon his message of love; it released the example and the power of *agape* in the world. As the chorus of the pop song by Malvina Reynolds, *The Magic Penny*, says:

Love is something if you give it away,
  give it away, give it away.
Love is something if you give it away;
  you end up having more.

# Summary

The word 'love' is in constant daily use, but it has a wide range of meanings; the English language is bereft of precise words. The Greek of New Testament times helps us to get closer to what Jesus and his friends meant by 'love'. 'God is love', John the Evangelist tells us (1 John 4:16), so when we encounter an unselfish loving act by another, we encounter God. The coming of God's kingdom, for which we pray daily in the Lord's Prayer, is brought about by such unselfish love for others. But the unselfish loving of others costs; it is difficult to separate love and suffering.

## *Bible reading*

John 3:11-18
(Alternative John 15:9-17)

# Discussion points

1. Had you ever thought about the various meanings of love before?

2. Do we all naturally know what love – as applied to God – really is or do you think discovering it is the task of a lifetime?

3. Are we really too blind to recognise Love (God) when we really meet it? (Any examples.)

4. Is it true that love and suffering are, as it were, two sides of the same coin?

5. As the Son of God loved us so deeply, was it inevitable that he should suffer?

6. If love causes us to suffer, can suffering be used in our daily prayer of love?

# Prayer

O God, I love Thee, I love Thee –
not out of hope of heaven for me
nor fearing not to love and be
in the everlasting burning.
Thou, Thou, my Jesus, after me
didst reach Thine arms out dying,
for my sake sufferedst nails and lance,
mocked and marred countenance,
sorrows passing number,
sweat and care and cumber,
yea and death, and this for me,
and Thou couldst see me sinning:
then I, why should not I love Thee,
Jesu, so much in love with me?
Not for heaven's sake; not to be
out of hell by loving Thee;
not for any gains I see;
but just the way that Thou didst me
I do love and I will love Thee:
what must I love Thee, Lord, for then?
For being my king and God.
Amen.

*Gerard Manley Hopkins*

# Fourth week of Lent

## Now is the kingdom

'Hurry up, we'll be late.' 'You haven't got your shoes on yet!' 'Have you been to the toilet?' 'Come on . . . I'm going without you.'

Getting a family of young children ready to go out, particularly to arrive on time somewhere, is a regular nightmare of frustration. Children have little concept of time and imagine that events only happen when *they* arrive; if, by chance, they arrive early they are indignant to know why they have to wait! We are all creatures of time. We 'take' it, 'save' it, 'spend' it and too often 'waste' it. Time moves relentlessly on with measured pace; yet seems to fly and when we are miserable it seems to drag. This ancient little verse can be seen in Chester Cathedral:

When as a child I laughed and wept – time crept.
When as a youth I dreamed and talked – time walked.
When I became a full-grown man – time ran.
And later as I older grew – time flew.
Soon we shall find while travelling on – time gone.
Will Christ have saved my soul by then? Amen.

'You've got lots of grey hairs coming, Dad,' Angela says, as I sit in the kitchen with a towel round my shoulders, having my hair cut by a proficient neighbour. 'Is it any wonder with the worries you children give me?' I reply with a laugh. 'Why don't you dye your hair?' Louise calls from the other side of the room. 'My hair's not that bad, Louise; anyway, I'm hoping to grow old gracefully.'

What is time? Some time ago there was a fascinating television programme on the BBC called *Sense of Timing*. It was a scientific enquiry into time, as viewed from the animal kingdom. It showed how relative time is. Of course, on earth the motion of the planet round its own axis and around the sun determines the length of the hour, the day and the year. The daily rhythm of plants, animals and humans is determined by the twenty-four-hour cycle of the sun.

*Sense of Timing* showed that time perception for a small creature, like a fly, is totally different from our own. To a fly the human world moves very slowly; a fly's reactions are ten times faster than ours. The programme makers contrasted the tiny elephantine shrew with a real elephant and demonstrated that body size determines the length of a life cycle and therefore the perception of time. The shrew lives a high-speed life with a heart rate of 600 beats per minute; the elephant, on the other hand, has a heart rate of twenty-four beats per minute! As most creatures have an average, all things being equal, of 800 million heartbeats in their life span, that means that the elephantine shrew lives for two-and-a-half years and the average elephant for sixty years.

Assuming *Sense of Timing* to be accurate, the larger the being the fewer the number of heartbeats, and the slower the perception of time. Is it not interesting for a person of faith to observe that the all-powerful, immeasurable spiritual being in the universe has no heartbeat and stands outside all time? Unless, of course, one could say that creation *is* the heartbeat of the Creator. There is only *now* for God and every moment is *now*.

The greatest minds in the history of Christianity have grappled with the concept of time. The great Augustine of Hippo asked 'What is time? If no one asks me, I know; but if I want to explain it to a questioner, I do not know.' He went on to add, 'If nothing passed there would be no past time; if nothing were approaching, there would be no future time; if nothing were, there would be no present time.' That seems fairly obvious; however, Augustine continues, 'But the two times, past and future, how can they *be*, since the past is no more, and the future is not yet? On the other hand, if the present were always present and never flowed away into the past, it would not be time at all, but eternity.'

This last observation is the thought we were exploring earlier; with God there is no time, just a continuous *now*. Augustine resumes with 'Perhaps it might be said that there are not three times, past, present and future, as we learned at school, but only the present because the other two do not exist . . . '*Confessions Book 11.*

Thomas Aquinas also philosophised about time and called it *nunc fluens* – the flowing *now*. That is just what time would seem to be for us, an ever-passing moment, a flowing *now*. As Augustine pointed out, it is only this present moment, now, which is real. Now is the only time there is. Now is the only real time we have or will ever have. St Paul was well aware of this truth. 'Now', he said, 'is the acceptable time, now is the day of salvation' (2 Corinthians 6:2).

When I have tried to explain time to my pupils, how it flows relentlessly on, composed of a continual stream of present moments, I have used a simple demonstration. I say, 'In a few moments' time, you won't know when until I actually do it, I'm going to click my thumb and second finger. You will hear a click.' I hold up my right hand for all to see. Expectancy is in the air. 'The click I will make in a minute or two lies some time in the future. You believe it is going to happen but you do not know precisely when. It is a future event.' There is a pause. Then I continue, 'When you hear the noise my finger and thumb will make, that will be the present moment, now.' Attention and anticipation fill the classroom and suddenly the 'click' is heard. I comment, 'You have just heard the sound; it has gone – it is now past. You can remember hearing it, in one passing *now* of time. And this is what time consists of. This is what your life and mine are made up of.'

Corrie Ten Boom, the famous Dutch Christian who, during World War II, was sent to a concentration camp, along with her father and sister, for hiding Jews in her home, grew up in a shop full of clocks. Her father was a watchmaker and she was the first woman in Holland officially licensed to follow the same trade. In one of her many books she tells the Dutch parable of the clock that had just been made and was put on a shelf between two old clocks. One of the old clocks said to the newcomer: 'So you have started out in life. I'm sorry for you. If you'll just think ahead and see how many ticks it takes to tick through one year, you will never make it. It would have been better had the maker never wound you up.'

So the clock began to count the ticks. 'Each second takes two ticks', he said to himself, 'which makes 120 ticks per minute. That's 7,200 ticks per hour', he calculated, '172,800 ticks per day; 1,209,600 ticks per week for the fifty-two weeks. That will make a total of 62,899,200 ticks per year. Horrors!' The clock immediately had a nervous breakdown and stopped ticking!

The wise old clock on the other side of him said 'Pay no attention to him. Just think. How many ticks do you have to tick at a time?'

' Why, only one, I suppose,' the new clock answered.

'There now. That's not so hard, is it? Try it along with me. Just one tick at a time!'

Seventy-five years later the clock was still ticking perfectly, one tick at a time.

Corrie Ten Boom adds the following to her story: 'Similarly, no man sinks under the burden of the day. It is only when yesterday's guilt is added to tomorrow's anxiety that our legs buckle and our backs break.'

In one moment of time a middle-aged Jew (in the first century AD, when life expectancy was so much shorter than our own, a man in his thirties would be middle-aged) late at night and alone in a garden, cried out to God, 'Abba, Father, everything is possible to you; take this suffering away from me; but not my will, your will be done' (Mark 14:36). Not many hours later the same man cried out in bitter torment, from the cross, 'My God, my God, why have you abandoned me?' Was this a prayer (Psalm 22:1) or a real sense of being deserted not only by his friends, but also by God?

For months and months the chief priests and the Herodians had plotted his death (Mark 3:6) and had set traps for him (Mark 3:1-6; Luke 20:20-26). The simplicity of the Gospel, 'Love God with your whole heart and your neighbour as yourself' (Luke 10:25-27) was too much in competition with the Rabbinical law-keeping. The tension built up. Jesus knew that they did not wish just to discredit him but to get rid of him. In one moment, perhaps the most important *now* of history, Jesus placed himself completely in God's hands; 'Not my will, your will be done.' And the next day it was.

Jesus of Nazareth was the embodiment of the Gospel. He truly loved God with his whole heart, he could not be untrue to his message and preaching. His Father did not directly will his Son's death but in the hours, minutes, before his arrest there were only two stark alternatives. Either give up preaching the disturbing Good News and disappear quietly from the scene or be faithful to the message of love and courageously face the consequences. The Father looked for faithfulness, trust and obedience.

The acceptance of his Father's wishes, that act of obedience, sprang directly from love. Without his faithfulness, trust and obedience the death the next day would have been nothing more than the judicial murder of an innocent man. These qualities sprang from the immense love within the heart of Jesus; there the kingdom of God was already established; there God reigned.

Some forty-five years ago a Christian poet, David Scott Blackhall, composed some verses on the Lord's Prayer. On the words 'Thy Kingdom come', he wrote: 'When I say "Thy Kingdom come", what do I understand by the Kingdom of

God? Where shall it come, when shall it come? Let it come first in our own hearts. A kingdom in any other place is beyond our comprehension. And we can put off, for the rest of our lives, a kingdom at any other time than now.'

## *Thy Kingdom come*

The sacred place of God is in a fourth
dimension of the heart. The hour of God
is in that other parallel of time
which we have learned to call eternity.
The place and hour meet at a point between
the thresholds of eternity and time,
the Sabbath on the brink of God's domain,
the everlasting unaccepted *now*.
If this cold fragment at the point of choice
stays in the heat and hate of life and time,
then it is lost for ever: if I lift
this mortal moment from the dust of time,
then God is in my heart and understanding,
and with this bounty has the Kingdom come.

Now there is a poem that deserves careful prayer and pondering! St Paul, I am sure, would welcome it as a suitable commentary upon his words, 'Now is the acceptable time, now is the day of salvation' (2 Corinthians 6:2).

'If I lift this mortal moment.' Surely that is what Jesus did continually in his daily life, compelled by his great love for the Father. The divine nature of Jesus showed not in his face, attractive personality though he certainly was, nor in his wonder-working (others had worked miracles) but in his loving. 'See how this man welcomes sinners and eats with them' (Luke 15:12).

Love can only be now: we cannot love in the past, it is dead,

46

and over that we have no control. We cannot love in the future; we hope that we will, when it arrives, but that too is not real. Now is the time for love, now is the time for God. The Kingdom comes *now* in our hearts by loving *now*, by being open to God and our neighbour *now*.

# Summary

We live in time and as we get older we are ever more conscious of its passing. The medieval theologian and saint, Thomas Aquinas, defined time as 'the flowing now'. The present moment is too precious to waste, it is the only reality that we have. We cannot live in the past or in the future, only now, in the present moment. 'Now' is the time for our salvation, Paul reminds his readers in Romans 13:8-14. Now is also the moment of the Kingdom; Jesus lived each mortal moment in the presence of his Father. We can do the same, and the Kingdom can come now in our hearts, by offering all that we are and do to the Father, as Jesus did.

## *Bible reading*

Romans 13:8-14
(Alternative reading Philippians 2:1-11)

# Discussion points

1. What are your thoughts on the passing of time? Does it seem to pass more swiftly now you are older?

2. Does the 'flowing now' adequately describe time?

3. Last week we discussed love. If we bring time and love together what are we led to understand about daily life?

4. Given that God is outside time, is the sacrifice of Calvary just a past historical event or does it have meaning and value now?

5. How can we apply Paul's words, 'Now is the acceptable time, now is the day of salvation' to our lives?

6. Is living the present moment to the full the only lesson we can take from our discussion this time?

# Prayer

Lord,
    you stretch at full length on the cross.
    There.
    Without a doubt, it is made for you.
    You cover it entirely, and you adhere to it more surely,
    you allow men to nail you carefully to it.
Lord,
    it was work well done, conscientiously done.
    Now you fit your Cross exactly, as the mechanic's
        carefully filed
    parts fit the engineer's blueprint.
    There had to be this precision.

Thus, Lord,
    I must gather my body, my heart, my spirit,
    and stretch myself on the Cross of this present moment.
    I haven't the right to choose the wood of my passion.
    The Cross is ready, to my measure.
    You present it to me each day, each minute, and I must
        lie on it.
    It isn't easy.
    The present moment is so limited that there isn't room
        to turn around.
And yet, Lord,
    I can meet you nowhere else.
    It's there that you await me.
    It's there that together we shall save our brothers.

from *Prayers on the Way of the Cross,* Michel Quoist

# Fifth week of Lent

## *The healing wounds of love*

According to reports received by the aid agencies and research carried out by the Anti-Slavery Society there are more people in slavery today than in 1883 when it was finally suppressed in the British Empire, and in 1865 when it was prohibited in North America! The Anti-Slavery Society has discovered that there are approximately 2,000,000 slaves in the world, the largest category being children who are sold and then grossly exploited at work.

One recent example is Binlah, an eleven-year-old girl from Thailand, whose story appeared in the British Sunday press. There are an estimated 5,000,000 child slaves in Thailand. Binlah originated from Korat, a poor village some 300 miles north of the capital, Bangkok. Her father sold her for the equivalent of eighty-five pounds to a recruiting agent who assured her parents that the girl would have a decent job in a restaurant. In fact she was re-sold to an ice-cream factory where she had to eat and sleep beside the ice-cream making machines and was brutally beaten and semi-starved. Her screams alerted neighbours and eventually their actions led to her release. She told her rescuers, 'I started work at 5 am and finished around midnight every day. The man used to hit me all the time to make me work faster. I was so tired. I cried a lot because I wanted to go home.'

Binlah is one of the lucky ones who escaped from the degradation of slavery. Tens of thousands of children in Thailand and other third world countries are worn out by the age of 16 and, useless to their owners, are abandoned to the slums which have grown up around Bangkok's gigantic mountains of city rubbish. They fall prey to drugs, alcoholism and cheap prostitution. These youngsters, made in the image and likeness of God, are reduced to total degradation and short brutal lives.

The economies of the Greek and Roman empires were largely built upon slavery. It was no different in the first century AD. The New Testament writers accepted slavery as a fact of daily life (see Ephesians 6:8 and Colossians 3:22). However, the foundations were gradually being laid, in the development and application of Christ's teaching, that would show that slavery was incompatible with the dignity of the children of God. 'You have clothed yourselves in Christ, and there are no more distinctions between Jew and Greek, slave and free, male and female, but all of you are one in Christ Jesus' (Galatians 3:28).

Writing to the Christians in Asia Minor, St Peter, in his first letter from Rome, covers several important topics. One of these is the encouragement he gives to slaves to bear patiently any harsh treatment or injustice they experience.

'Christ suffered for you and left an example for you to follow the way he took. He had not done anything wrong . . . he was insulted and did not retaliate with insults; when he was tortured he made no threats but he put his trust in the righteous judge. He was bearing our faults in his own body on the Cross, so that we might die to our faults and live for holiness; by his wounds you have been healed' (1 Peter 2:22-24).

Does Peter mean that when we suffer an injustice we should not speak up in our own defence? Is it more perfect patiently to bear some wrong done to us in silence, as Jesus did, and simply trust God, the righteous judge, to sort the future out in his own good time? This is a problem that serious Christians sometimes face.

Peter here encourages Christians who are slaves to gain some spiritual benefit from their condition. However, with the passing of time, the improvement of social conditions in the West and, above all, the working of the Holy Spirit, we now appreciate that, while there is much spiritual value in patient endurance, injustice and inequality have to be fought. We are so much more aware of human rights and that it is our Christian duty to speak out and work for social justice.

A wonderful tribute to twentieth century Christian martyrs stands clear for all to see in the very centre of London. Ten stone statues now fill the niches on the gothic west front of Westminster Abbey which have stood empty since the Middle Ages. They are in the company of the Virgin Mary and St John the Evangelist. The ten, from different Christian traditions from around the world, including Anglican, Orthodox and Catholic, were selected because of their 'openness to death for the glory of Christ'.

At first there was hesitancy about including, for example, Martin Luther King and Oscar Romero, because they had not strictly speaking died for their Christian faith; technically they had not been killed by *odium fidei* (hatred of the faith). However, theologians pointed out that they had been killed by *odium iustitiae* (hatred of justice), and we now understand that a hatred of justice is as much a hatred of God as is a hatred of the Christian faith. So, at the heart of London, proudly presented for all to see, are tributes to men and women who have stood up to injustice and evil.

The story of Martin Luther King and his assassination in the struggle for equal rights for black Americans is well known. Oscar Romero, the archbishop of El Salvador, spoke out bravely and continually against the injustices that the poor suffered in his country at the hands of a ruthless National Security government, professedly Christian. He was assassinated while saying Mass on 24 March 1980. Two weeks before he was martyred he spoke in an interview about the death threats he had received and his expectation that he would be killed. 'If God accepts the sacrifice of my life, then may my blood be the seed of liberty and a sign that hope will soon become a reality.' Later in the interview he said, 'Can you tell them, if they succeed in killing me, that I pardon and bless those who do it. But I wish that they could realise that they are wasting their time. A bishop may die but the Church of God, which is the people, will never die'.

We need examples like these because we so easily and weakly take refuge in pious words, rather than taking positive action. Little Binlah, crouched for the night beside the ice-making machines, would receive no benefit from a do-gooder telling her, 'Be patient, Child, accept the cross laid upon you; it is God's will'. Such an evil injustice inflicted upon an innocent child could never be the will of her heavenly Father.

I have long admired Edward England, a well-respected editor in Christian publishing, and an author. Years ago, on seeing on the television news the reports of the terrible disaster at Aberfan in Wales, when hundreds of little school children were buried alive in their school, he got up from his armchair, went upstairs and packed a bag. 'Where are you going?' his wife asked. 'I'm going to help', Edward replied; and within thirty minutes of seeing the news report, he was on the train to Wales. Within hours, and for days, he was there, digging with his hands, alongside hundreds of other volunteers.

We are never likely to change things or grow spiritually as Christ would have us grow if, when faced with injustice, we resort to empty words and excuses. Only action, however simple, will bring about change.

In their book, *Introducing Liberation Theology*, Leonardo and Clodovis Boff tell of an incident which changed forever a certain bishop's approach to injustice.

> One day, in the arid region of north-eastern Brazil, one of the most famine-stricken parts of the world, I (Clodovis Boff) met a bishop going into his house; he was shaking. 'Bishop, what's the matter?' I asked. He replied that he had just seen a terrible sight. In front of the Cathedral was a woman with three small children and a baby clinging to her neck. He saw that they

were fainting from hunger. The baby seemed to be dead. He said, 'Give the baby some milk, woman!'

'I can't, my Lord,' she answered.

The bishop went on insisting that she should and she said that she could not. Finally, because of his insistence, she opened her blouse. Her breast was bleeding; the baby sucked violently at it and sucked blood. The mother who had given it life was feeding it, like the pelican, with her own blood, her own life. The bishop knelt down in front of the woman, placed his hand on the baby's head and there and then vowed that, as long as such hunger existed, he would feed at least one hungry child each day.

That was a particularly dramatic example, not within the scope of most of us. However, action by each of us who have faith is always possible.

Tomorrow, as I write, Saturday 22 August, at 3.10 pm, there will be a one minute silence observed throughout Ireland for the twenty-eight victims of the bomb outrage at Omagh, Co. Tyrone, murdered a week ago. Since the stunning and shocking news first broke, and as, this week, the youngsters and other family members who died have been buried, people have felt such sympathy for those who grieve. Our loving concern, on occasions like this, prompts us to want to do something. In love, all we have been able to do, in spirit, is to stand alongside those who hurt so deeply, with constant prayer for them. Our faith tells us how valuable such action is.

For a husband with three very young children to be robbed by a terrorist's bomb of his wife and baby daughter *feels* like a terrible injustice to him. Peter's words on patient endurance may be the last thing that he wants to hear; but the truth is that Jesus suffered unjustly too, and he is *the* model of such patience. He knew what it was to be innocent of any wrongdoing, yet forced to suffer cruelly and unjustly. Intense grief is an unwanted slavery, as is unjust treatment.

If the injustice suffered comes from church authorities we

need to recall that Jesus was unjustly found guilty by the High Priest and the Jewish ecclesiastical apparatus of his time. If the injustice is from the State, or local authorities, there is no better image to hold in one's imagination than Jesus standing before the weak and vacillating Pilate; if the injury is caused by family or friends, there is the memory of Judas, and Peter saying 'I do not even know the man'.

Humanly Jesus was a powerless victim of injustice, as Isaiah says: 'Like a lamb that is led to the slaughterhouse, like a sheep that is dumb before its shearers . . . he was pierced through for our faults' (Isaiah 53:7-8).

It was not just the immense patience of Christ that Peter commended to us, there was also his obedience. Jesus accepted the consequence of his preaching. He believed his Father expected him to be faithful and be obedient even to the death reserved for runaway slaves, the cross.

To gain her freedom from the proprietor of the ice-cream factory Binlah had to be bought back or redeemed by those trying to save her; a ransom had to be paid for her. The New Testament writers, in trying to explain what it was that Jesus did for us by dying on the cross, employ a wide variety of words and concepts. *Salvation* is a word rich in meaning and cannot be explained simply by just one set of words, but one of the metaphors used is taken from the buying back, or redemption, of slaves. To buy us back from the slavery of sin, St Peter suggests the idea in his letter that Jesus paid the price of the blood that flowed from his wounds. 'Remember, the ransom that was paid to free you from the useless way of life your ancestors handed down was not paid in anything corruptible, neither silver nor gold, but in the precious blood of a lamb without spot or stain, namely Christ' (1 Peter 1:18-19).

Crucifixion was the death reserved for runaway slaves and political agitators. Jesus tried desperately hard not to be thought of and accepted as a political Messiah, yet it was on a trumped-up political charge that Pilate condemned him. What Jesus did try to do was to view himself and his ministry as *servant*, modelling himself upon the Servant of God portrayed in the prophetic Servant Songs of Isaiah. It was the death penalty of a bad, runaway slave that he suffered, as a ransom for all who are enslaved by injustice or guilty of causing injustices.

The Five Wounds of Jesus are signs of the love and obedience of the Suffering Servant, and it is a share in that healing love and that healing obedience that we, who look upon the crucifix, need.

# Summary

Slavery is not a thing of the past; there are more slaves today than there were when slavery was outlawed in the late nineteenth century. Jesus knew families that had slaves and Paul, in his letters, encourages slaves to accept their condition patiently. By the light and guidance of the Holy Spirit we now realise that human dignity and the applied teaching of Jesus condemn all forms of social injustice. Christian heroes of the twentieth century, martyrs who have had 'an openness to death for the glory of Christ' have pointed the way. Christ is our model in coping with and facing up to injustice.

*Bible reading*

Mark 10:35-45
(Alternative reading James 1:19-27)

# Discussion points

1. Are you surprised by the statistics about modern slavery?
   Are there more forms of 'slavery' in our own society?

2. Is it more Christian to suffer an injustice in silence and with
   patience than to stand up and fight?

3. Are we being political if we stand up for those who are
   oppressed by injustice, either in our own country or abroad?

4. How does slavery today relate to the wounds of Christ?

5. Are the wounds of the suffering Christ or the risen Christ a source of healing for ourselves and society? How?

6. Can you summarise in a few words what you have learned from our Lenten Course and perhaps share any resolutions you have made?

# Prayer

Lord,
    we pray this day
    mindful of the sorry confusion of our world.
Look with mercy upon this generation of your children,
    so steeped in misery of their own contriving,
    so far strayed from your ways and so blinded by passions.
We pray for the victims of tyranny,
    that they may resist oppression with courage.
We pray for the wicked and cruel men
    whose arrogance reveals to us
    what the sin of our own hearts is like,
    when it has conceived and brought forth its final fruit.

We pray for ourselves
    who live in peace and quietness,
    that we may not regard our good fortune
    as proof of our virtue,
    or rest content to have our ease
    at the price of other men's sorrow and tribulation.

We pray for all
    who have some vision of your will
    despite the confusions and betrayals of human sin,
    that they may humbly and resolutely plan for and fashion
    the foundations of a just peace between men,
    even while they seek to preserve
    what is fair and just among us
    against the threat of malignant powers.

*Reinhold Niebuhr*

# Acknowledgements

Scriptural quotations are taken from the Jerusalem Bible, published by Darton, Longman and Todd.

The publishers wish to express their gratitude to the following for permission to include copyright material in this book:

Association Diocesaine du Havre, 17 Rue Percanville, Le Havre, France, for the *Prayer on the Way of the Cross* by Michel Quoist, published by Gill & MacMillan, Dublin, 1965.

Burns & Oates, Wellwood, North Farm Road, Tunbridge Wells, Kent, TN2 3DR, for the extract from *Introducing Liberation Theology* by Leonardo and Clodovis Boff.

MCA Music Ltd, Elsinore House, 77 Fulham Palace Road, London, W6 8JA, for the extract from *The Magic Penny* by Malvina Reynolds, © Copyright 1955 MCA Music Ltd.

SCM Press Ltd, 9-17 St Albans Place, London, N1 0NX, for the extract from *New Testament Words* by William Barclay, SCM Press 1964.

Every effort has been made to trace the owners of copyright material and we hope that no copyright has been infringed. Pardon is sought and apology is made if the contrary be the case and a correction will be made in any reprint of this book.